Pebble™ Plus

Sports and Activities

Let's Play Baseball!

by Terri DeGezelle

Consulting Editor: Gail Saunders-Smith, PhD

Consultant: Kymm Ballard, MA
Physical Education, Athletics, and Sports Medicine Consultant
North Carolina Department of Public Instruction

Capstone press

Mankato, Minnesota

Pebble Plus is published by Capstone Press,
151 Good Counsel Drive, P.O. Box 669, Mankato, Minnesota 56002.
www.capstonepress.com

1 2 3 4 5 6 11 10 09 08 07 06

Library of Congress Cataloging-in-Publication Data
DeGezelle, Terri, 1955–
  Let's play baseball! / by Terri DeGezelle.
    p. cm. — (Pebble plus. Sports and activities)
    Includes bibliographical references and index.
    ISBN-13: 978-0-7368-5361-3 (hardcover)
    ISBN-10: 0-7368-5361-8 (hardcover)
    1. Baseball—Juvenile literature. I. Title. II. Series.
  GV867.5.D44 2006
  796.357—dc22
                                    2005017944

Summary: Simple text and photographs present the skills, equipment, and safety concerns of playing baseball.

Editorial Credits
Heather Adamson, editor; Kia Adams, designer; Kelly Garvin, photo researcher

Photo Credits
All photos Capstone Press/ TJ Thoraldson Digital Photography except page 13, Getty Images/Jake Rajs and
    page 15, Corbis/David Madison/zefa.

The author thanks Chris Biehn for sharing his knowledge of baseball.

Note to Parents and Teachers

The Sports and Activities set supports national physical education standards related
to recognizing movement forms and exhibiting a physically active lifestyle. This book
describes and illustrates baseball. The images support early readers in understanding the
text. The repetition of words and phrases helps early readers learn new words. This book
also introduces early readers to subject-specific vocabulary words, which are defined in
the Glossary section. Early readers may need assistance to read some words and to use
the Table of Contents, Glossary, Read More, Internet Sites, and Index sections of the book.

Table of Contents

Playing Baseball

Catch, throw, hit, run, score!

Friends play baseball together.

Teams take turns at bat.

The pitcher throws the ball.

The batter tries to hit the ball

with a bat.

Batters run to bases after
they hit the ball.
They score runs
by touching all the bases.

The fielding team tries to

catch the batted ball.

They throw it.

They try to tag

the runner out.

Equipment

Baseball fields have three
bases and a home plate.
They make a diamond shape.

Baseball bats are made from
strong wood or metal.
They are built tough
to hit baseballs hard.

Safety

Players wear helmets
to protect their heads.
They also wear caps to shield
their eyes from the sun.

Players use leather gloves
to catch baseballs.
Then the ball does not hurt
their hands.

Having Fun

Come hit the ball and

run the bases.

Let's play baseball!

Glossary

base—a bag or plate marking one of the four corners of a baseball diamond; runners must make it around all the bases without getting tagged out to score a run.

diamond—a shape with four equal sides and two pairs of angles; baseball diamonds are actually squares that look like diamonds.

out—ending a batter's attempt to score by catching a batter's hit, tagging a runner with the ball, or throwing the ball to a base before the runner reaches it; after three outs, the teams switch batting and fielding.

pitcher—the player who throws the ball over home plate; in beginning leagues, a coach may be the pitcher.

protect—to keep safe

Read More

Fauchald, Nick. *Nice Hit!: You Can Play Baseball.* Game Day. Minneapolis: Picture Window Books, 2004.

Gibbons, Gail. *My Baseball Book.* New York: HarperCollins, 2000.

Klingel, Cynthia, and Robert B. Noyed. *Baseball.* Wonder Books. Chanhassen, Minn.: Child's World, 2001.

Internet Sites

FactHound offers a safe, fun way to find Internet sites related to this book. All of the sites on FactHound have been researched by our staff.

Here's how:

1. Visit *www.facthound.com*

2. Type in this special code **0736853618** for age-appropriate sites. Or enter a search word related to this book for a more general search.

3. Click on the **Fetch It** button.

FactHound will fetch the best sites for you!

Index

Word Count: 140
Grade: 1
Early-Intervention Level: 13